Newport Community Learning & Libraries

X022550

D0494099

STAR WARS™

WORKBOOKS

SHAPES, COLOURS & PATTERNS

FOR AGES 4–5

BY THE EDITORS OF BRAIN QUEST
EDUCATIONAL CONSULTANT: CHARLOTTE RABY

SCHOLASTIC

Newport Community Learning
& Libraries

X022550

PETERS	15-Mar-2018
J510	£5.99

Scholastic Children's Books
Euston House,
24 Eversholt Street,
London NW1 1DB, UK

A division of Scholastic Ltd
London ~ New York ~ Toronto ~ Sydney ~ Auckland
Mexico City ~ New Delhi ~ Hong Kong

First published in the USA by Workman Publishing in 2014.
This edition published in the UK by Scholastic Ltd in 2016.
© & TM 2016 LUCASFILM LTD.

STAR WARS is a registered trademark of Lucasfilm Ltd.
BRAIN QUEST is a registered trademark of Workman Publishing Co., Inc., and Groupe Play Bac, S.A.

Workbook series design by Raquel Jaramillo
Cover illustration by Mike Sutfin
Interior illustrations by Bret Blevins

ISBN 978 1407 16290 4

Printed in Malaysia

2 4 6 8 10 9 7 5 3 1

All rights reserved

This book is sold subject to the condition that it shall not, by way of trade or otherwise be lent, resold, hired out, or
otherwise circulated without the publisher's prior consent in any form or binding other than that in which it is published
and without a similar condition, including this condition, being imposed upon the subsequent purchaser.

Papers used by Scholastic Children's Books are made from woods grown in sustainable forests.

www.scholastic.co.uk

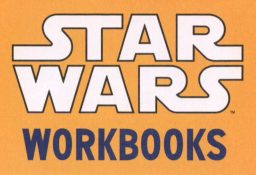

WORKBOOKS

This workbook belongs to:

_____

Circle ⬤

A **circle** is round.

Trace the **circle**.

Draw a face inside the **circle**.

Now draw your own **circle** in the space below.

Find the Ewoks

The Ewok needs help finding his friends.

Follow the path of **circles** to help him find his way.

Circles!

How many **circles** can you find?

Point to all the **circles** in the picture.

Rectangle

A **rectangle** has four sides.

Two sides are long. Two sides are short.

Trace the **rectangle**.

Draw a picture inside the **rectangle**.

Now draw your own **rectangle** in the space below.

Find the Sith

Help Darth Sidious find Darth Vader.

Follow the path of **rectangles** to help him find his way.

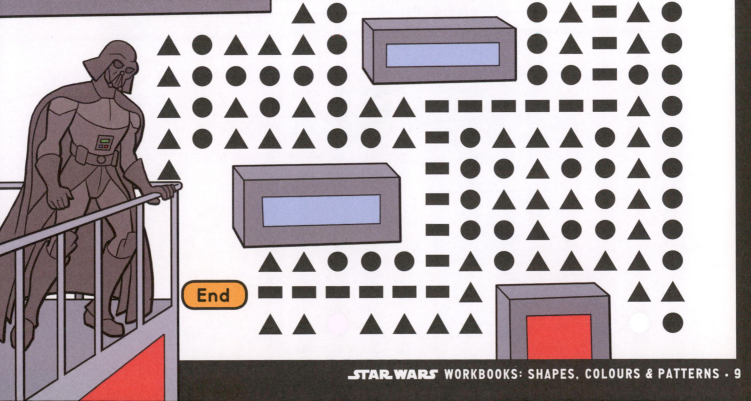

Rectangles!

How many **rectangles** can you find?

Point to all the **rectangles** in the picture.

Square

A **square** has four equal sides.

Trace the **square**.

Draw a house using the **square**.

Now draw your own **square** in the space below.

Find the Fort

Help the Rebel trooper find his fort.

Follow the path of **squares** to help him find his way.

Start

End

Squares!

How many **squares** can you find?

Point to all the **squares** in the picture.

Triangle ▲

A **triangle** has three sides.

Trace the **triangle**.

Draw a picture using the **triangle**.

Now draw your own **triangle** in the space below.

Find the Band

The musician needs help finding his band.

Follow the path of **triangles** to help him find his way.

Triangles!

How many **triangles** can you find?

Point to all the **triangles** in the picture.

Red

red

Colour the lightsaber **red**.

Colour Darth Maul **red**.

Colour the Imperial Guards **red**.

Orange

orange

Colour the planet Bespin **orange**.

Colour Nute Gunray's tunic **orange**.

Colour the Royal Handmaidens' gowns **orange**.

Yellow

yellow

Colour C-3PO **yellow**.

Colour the sun **yellow**.

Colour the Naboo starfighters **yellow**.

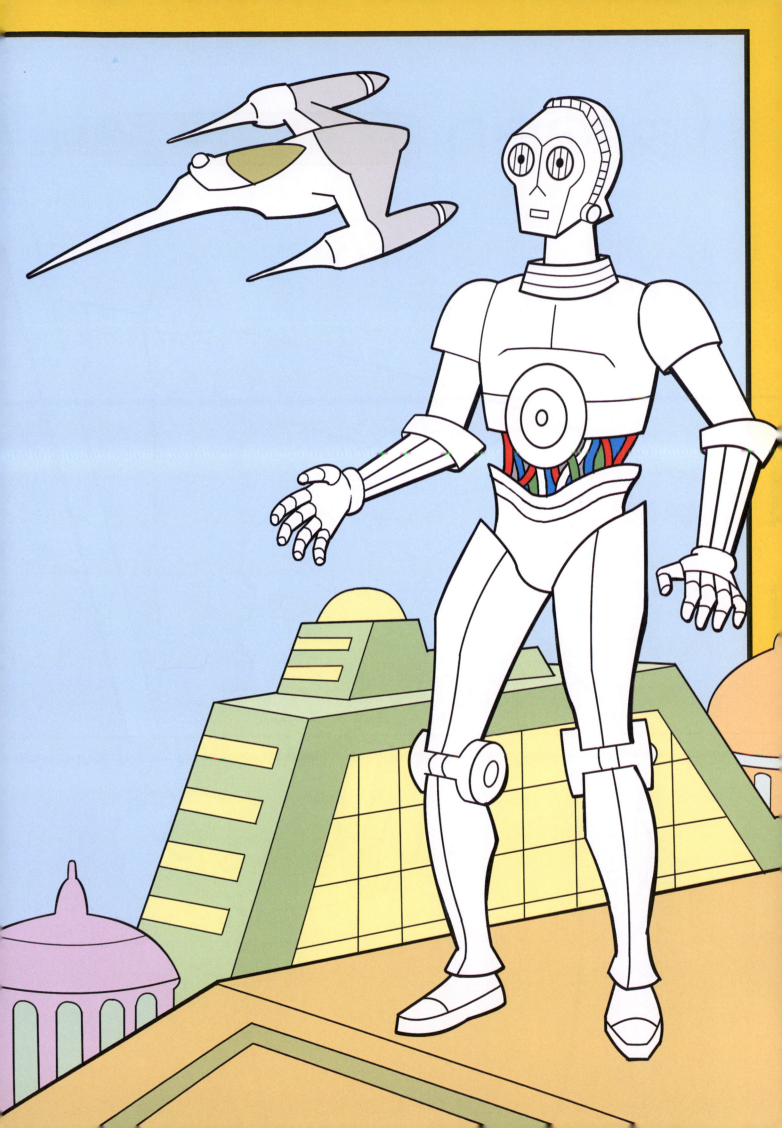

Green

green

Colour the lightsabers **green**.

Colour Luminara Unduli **green**.

Colour the acklay **green**.

Colour Yoda **green**.

Blue

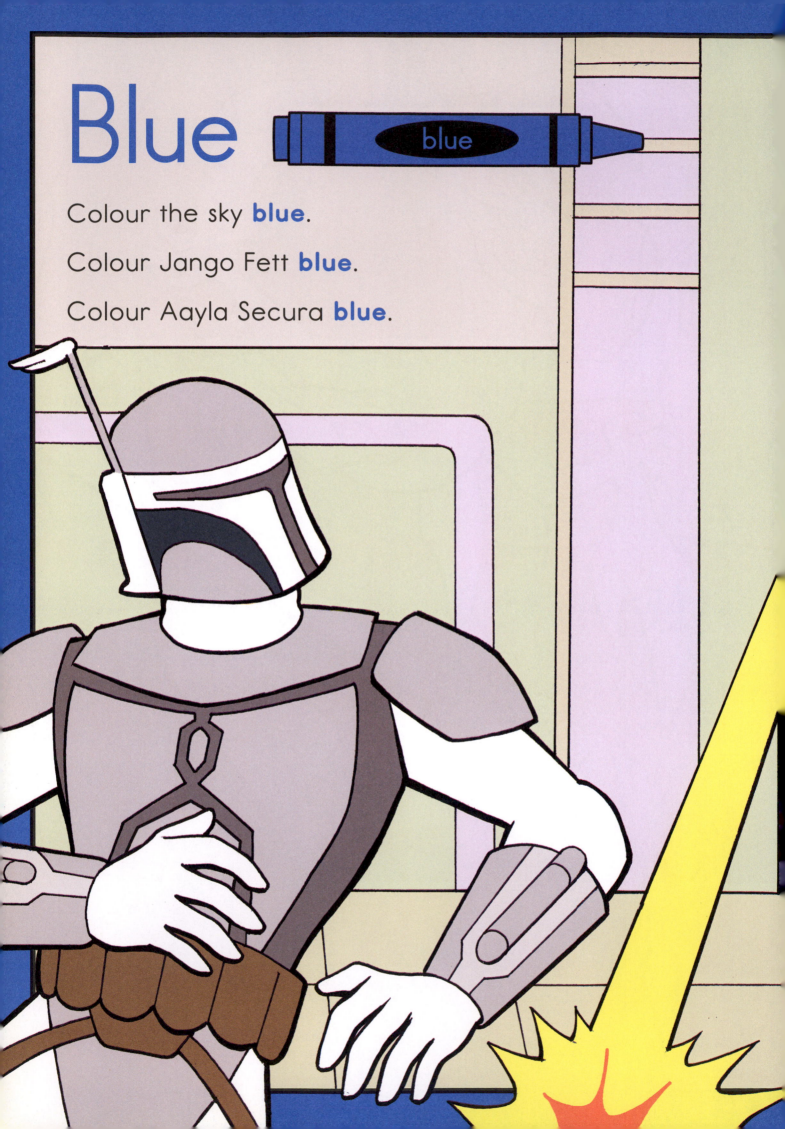

Colour the sky **blue**.

Colour Jango Fett **blue**.

Colour Aayla Secura **blue**.

Purple

purple

Colour the podracer **purple**.

Colour the Kaminoan **purple**.

Colour the crystals **purple**.

Brown

Colour the Wookiee **brown**.

Colour the tree trunk **brown**.

Colour the Ewoks **brown**.

Black

black

Colour Darth Vader **black**.

Colour the Emperor **black**.

Colour Luke Skywalker **black**.

Grey

grey

Colour the Star Destroyers **grey**.

Colour the Death Star **grey**.

Colour the TIE fighters **grey**.

White

white

Colour the scout trooper **white**.

Colour the stormtrooper **white**.

Colour the clouds **white**.

Rainbow

Help Anakin colour the rainbow.

red

orange

yellow

green

blue

indigo

violet

Mos Espa Market!

Colour the **1** sky **blue**.

Colour the **2** suns **yellow**.

Colour the **3** landspeeders **red**.

Colour the **4** stormtroopers **white**.

Colour the **5** starships **grey**.

Colour the **6** fruit **purple**.

Colour the **7** windows **black**.

Colour the **8** Jawas **brown**.

Colour the **9** flowers **orange**.

Colour the **10** bottles **green**.

Guess Who?

Who is hiding in this picture?

Colour the shapes with **B** **brown**.

Colour the shapes with **O** **orange**.

Guess Who?

Who is hiding in this picture?

Colour the shapes with **B blue**.

Colour the shapes with **G grey**.

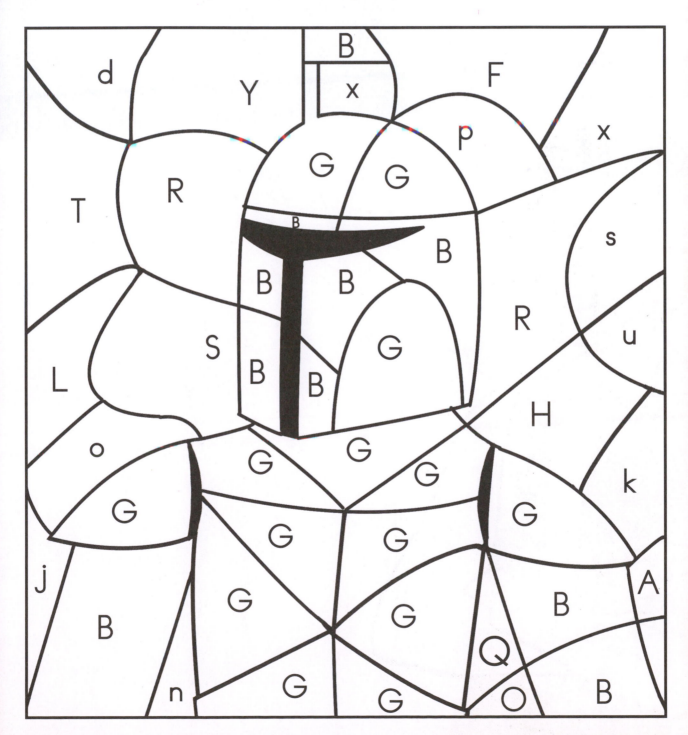

Star

Can you see the shape of a star?

Colour it **yellow**.

Heart

Can you see the shape of a heart?

Colour it **red**.

Yoda's Blanket

Can you colour the blanket in?

Colour the circles **purple**.

Colour the squares **blue**.

Colour the rectangles **green**.

Colour the triangles **orange**.

Colour the hearts **red**.

Colour the stars **yellow**.

Planets!

Can you see a **pattern** in the colours of the planets?

Colour the last planet in the row with the colour you think comes next.

Droids!

Look for the **pattern** in the droids.

Circle the droid that should come next.

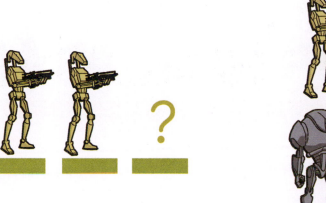

Starships!

Look for the **pattern** in the starships.

Circle the starship that should come next.

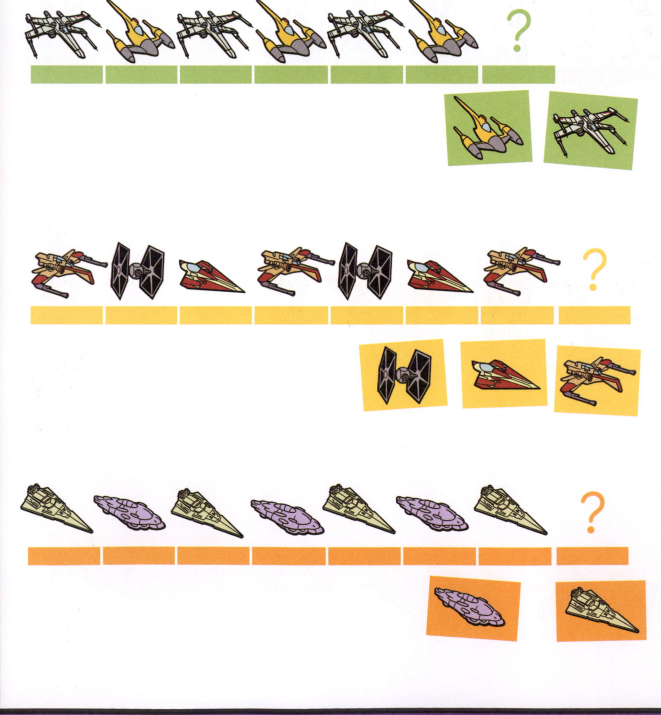

Lightsabers!

Draw a line between the cards that have the **same** number of lightsabers on them.

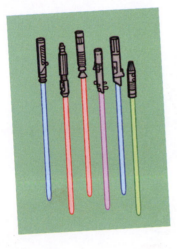

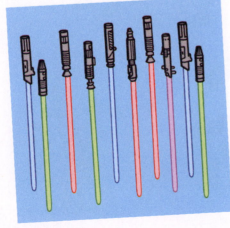

The Same

Look at each group of objects.

Circle two objects that are the **same** on each card.

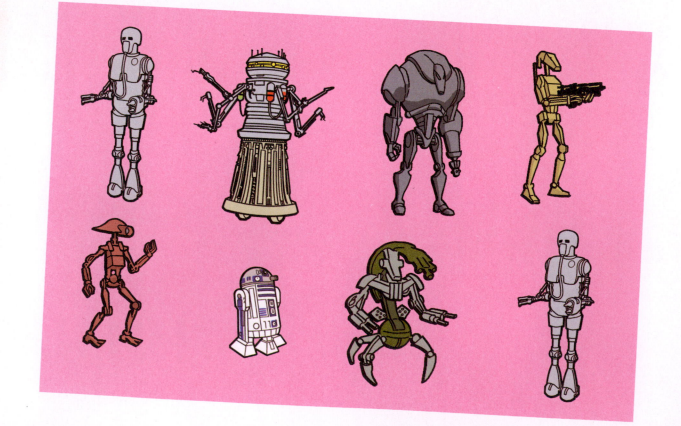

Different

Look at each group of characters.

Circle the one who is **different** from the others in the group.

Ewoks!

Look at each group of Ewoks.

Circle the Ewok who is **different** from the others in the group.

Look at this page of Ewoks.

All of the Ewoks have an exact match.

Draw a line between each pair of Ewoks who
are exactly the **same**.

Clone Troopers!

Look at this page of clone troopers.

Circle the two clone troopers that are exactly the **same**.

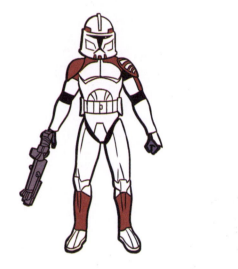

Look at this page of clone troopers.

All the clone troopers have an exact match except for one.

Draw a line between each pair of clone troopers that are exactly the **same**.

Draw a circle around the clone trooper that is **different** from all of the others.

Fix It!

Anakin is building a droid.

Circle the two tools below that Anakin can use to build a droid.

Friends!

Look at the pictures on each group of cards.

Circle the two characters who are friends in each group.

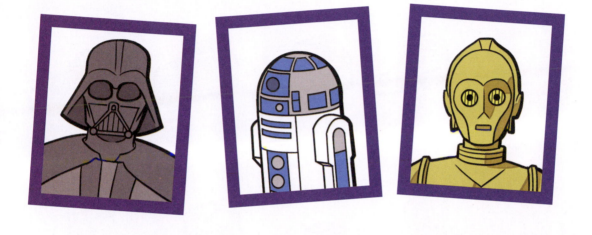

Pairs!

Two shoes that look alike make a pair.

Circle the shoe in each row that makes a pair with the shoe on the card.

Things That Fly!

Circle all the things that can fly.

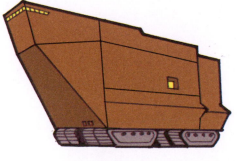

So Silly!

Something is wrong with these pictures.

Draw an X on the thing that does not belong in each picture.

Galactic Dots!

The aim of the game is to make the most squares. Take turns to draw a line between the dots. The player who makes the fourth line of the square wins the square. Mark the square you win with the first letter of your name.

Game 1

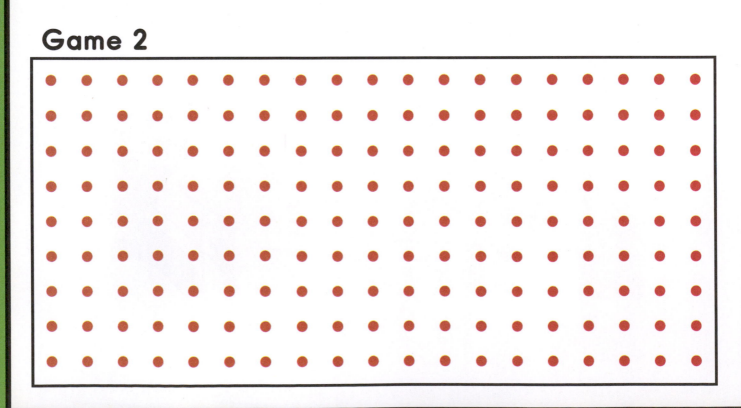

Game 2

Game 3

Death Star!

Look at the Death Star.

Circle the piece that is missing.

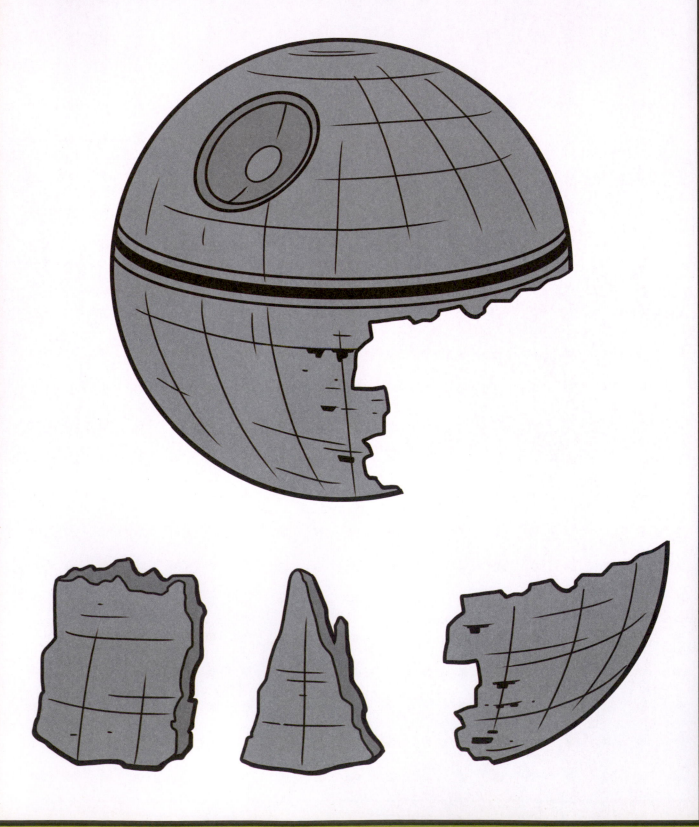

Mustafar

Help Obi-Wan escape the volcano.

Draw a line connecting the **red** circles that show which path he should take.

End

Start

Race

Help Anakin win the race by taking the fastest path.

Draw a line connecting the **orange** rectangles that show which path he should take.

Start

End

FINISH

Cloud City

Help Han Solo get to Cloud City.

Draw a line connecting the **yellow** rectangles that show which path he should take.

End

Start →

R2-D2

Help R2-D2 get to the starfighter.

Draw a line connecting the **blue** squares that show which path he should take.

Escape

Help Princess Leia escape the stormtroopers.

Draw a line connecting the **purple** squares that show which path she should take.

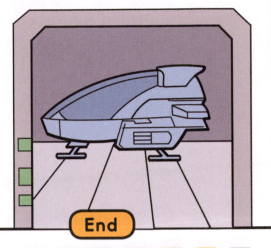

End

Start

Run, Luke!

Help Luke run to the stairs.

Draw a line connecting the **black** triangles that show which path he should take.

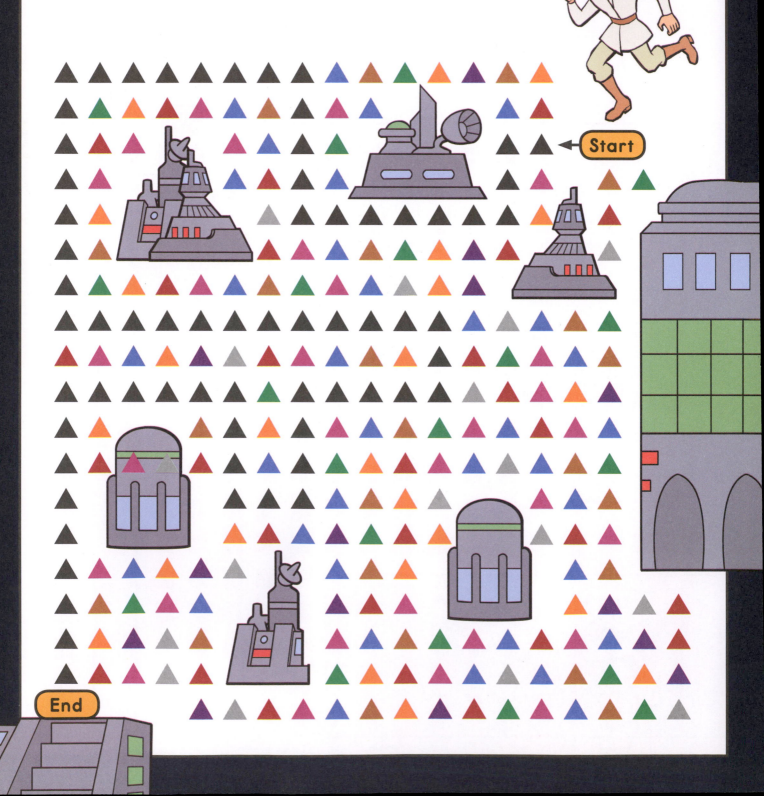

Jabba's Palace

Help C-3PO escape Jabba the Hutt's palace.

Draw a line connecting the **brown** triangles that show which path he should take.

Start

End

Starfighter

Help the X-wing starfighter reach the moon.

Draw a line connecting the **grey** stars that show which path it should take.

Start

End

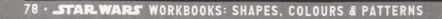

Naboo Ocean

Help the Gungan submarine reach the underwater city.

Draw a line connecting the **green** hearts that show which path it should take.

Duel!

Obi-Wan Kenobi and Darth Vader are in a lightsaber duel.

Colour the picture in.

The Force!

Yoda is teaching Luke Skywalker how to use the Force.

Colour the picture in.

Anakin and Padmé

Anakin and Padmé are having a picnic.

Colour the picture in.

Best Friends!

Luke, Leia and Han are talking to Chewbacca, R2-D2 and C-3PO.

Colour the picture in.

The Battle!

Mace Windu, Agen Kolar, Saesee Tiin and Kit Fisto battle Emperor Palpatine.

Colour the picture in.

Now you know your shapes, colours and patterns!

Are you ready to have more fun with *Star Wars*?

Let's make some finger puppets!

Using the templates on the following pages, ask an adult to help you follow the instructions to cut, fold and glue together finger-puppet versions of *Star Wars* characters.

What you need:

- Finger-puppet templates

- Safety scissors

- Sticky tape or glue

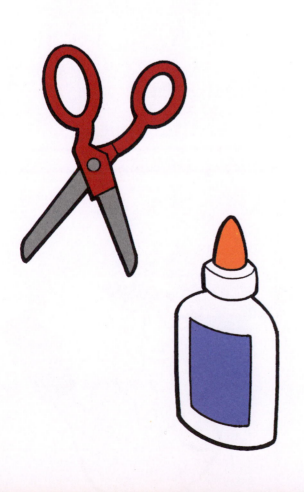

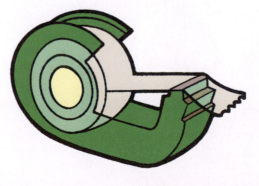

Finger Puppets

1 Ask an adult to cut out each finger puppet.

2 Curve the rectangular piece at the bottom of each puppet.

3 Ask an adult to tape or glue together the yellow marked areas.

4 Place finger puppets on your fingers!

Star Wars Workbooks: Shapes, Colours & Patterns
Scholastic Ltd
©LFL

Star Wars Workbooks: Shapes, Colours & Patterns
Scholastic Ltd
©LFL

Star Wars Workbooks: Shapes, Colours & Patterns
Scholastic Ltd
©LFL

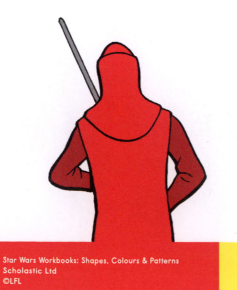

Star Wars Workbooks: Shapes, Colours & Patterns
Scholastic Ltd
©LFL

Star Wars Workbooks: Shapes, Colours & Patterns
Scholastic Ltd
©LFL

TH 16/3/18

Star Wars Workbooks: Shapes, Colours & Patterns
Scholastic Ltd
©LFL

Star Wars Workbooks: Shapes, Colours & Patterns
Scholastic Ltd
©LFL

Star Wars Workbooks: Shapes, Colours & Patterns
Scholastic Ltd
©LFL

Star Wars Workbooks: Shapes, Colours & Patterns
Scholastic Ltd
©LFL

Star Wars Workbooks: Shapes, Colours & Patterns
Scholastic Ltd
©LFL